Excel for Budgeting

M.L. HUMPHREY

CONTENTS

CONTENTS (CONT.)

CONTENTS (CONT.)

INTRODUCTION

I'm a huge advocate of using Microsoft Excel because I've found it invaluable in my professional life. It has uses for individuals as well, though, and the most significant of those, in my opinion, is for budgeting and personal finances.

In *Budgeting for Beginners* I laid out my approach to budgeting and personal finances, including how to judge your financial health and how to improve on your current situation. Underlying the material covered in *Budgeting for Beginners* was certain calculations about how much you own, owe, earn, and spend as well as what your short-term liquid net worth is.

At the time I published the first edition of that book I also published *Juggling Your Finances: Basic Excel Primer* which walked a new user to Excel through how to calculate those basic measures. It was essentially how to do addition, subtraction, multiplication, and division in Excel using budgeting examples.

But what that book didn't do was pull everything together in the way my own tracking workbook does. This is something that I've used for close to a decade now that has evolved as I've refined how to easily track my finances and analyze my current situation. And as someone who is self-employed and tends to make financially bold choices, I've needed to be on top of my finances to keep going.

So that's what this book is intended to do. We're going to build a workbook just like the one I use for my own finances that gives you a nice snapshot of where you are financially on one page with some additional calculations thrown in on other worksheets. Once you create this document it will become a living, breathing view of your current financial situation that you should keep updated at least monthly if not more often. (I usually update the month-to-date numbers at least weekly and the debt and non-bank asset balances monthly.)

If you're not familiar with Excel this may be a little overwhelming to work through. It is mostly basic math (addition, subtraction, multiplication, division), but there's also some conditional formatting and I use the SUMIFS functions more than once. There's also some formatting to make it all pretty.

In the Appendices I have provided basic overviews of how to do all of these things, but the appendices are not meant to teach just provide a refresher.

I do provide step-by-step instructions for how to create all of this. But since I don't know your numbers I have to do it with sample data. Which means you will have to be comfortable enough in Excel to adjust what I have in the examples to meet your own needs. Hopefully I've explained it all thoroughly enough so that you can do that, but if you get stuck you can always reach out to me and I'm happy to answer your questions.

(I won't build your worksheet for you, but I will explain how things work if something isn't clear.)

We'll start this book by covering basic Excel terminology and then we're going to just dive into creating the various components. Each one will have an overview section where we discuss what we're building and then a build section where there are numbered steps for you to walk through. If you're shaky on Excel and finances, I'd suggest building the examples exactly as I have them here and then making changes to accommodate your own situation. If you "get it" from the overview discussion, then just build each one with your own information instead. But for those trying to work their way into this, it's probably best to just build the examples to start. That way you have something to compare against.

By the time we're done here, you will have:

• A monthly payment tracker that shows which bills you owe, which have already been paid, and how much you still owe for the month.

• A cash and credit card spending tracker where you can track your expenses that are paid for using cash or a credit card each month by category so that you can see if your actual spending matches your budget for that category.

• A listing of your current liquid assets (cash and non-restricted bank accounts) and a three-month projection of income and expenses for each month to see where you'll be financially over the next three months.

• A listing of your assets, including haircuts on each asset to allow the calculation of a liquid value for those assets.

• A listing of your liabilities.

• A calculation of your net worth and liquid net worth.

• A listing of your available credit.

• A calculation of your short-term liquid net worth and long-term liquid net worth.

Introduction

- For the self-employed, a receivables tracker that looks at money you're owed and money you've received for the year. (Also includes tracking of payments in multiple currencies.)

- A two-variable analysis grid for scenario analysis.

If you're familiar with finances you can use this guide without having read *Budgeting for Beginners*. Just know that there are certain topics that I discuss in both books, such as haircutting your assets and the importance of short-term liquid net worth, that I cover in more detail in *Budgeting for Beginners*.

Also, if you'd rather not go through the detailed work of creating the template from scratch yourself, you can go to https://payhip.com/mlhumphrey and download the Excel template (the *Excel for Budgeting Excel Template*) that was used to create the screenshots in this book for 99 cents. It will still need to be customized to you and your information, but using it may save you some time.

Alright then. Let's dive in and get started with building a simple payment tracker for tracking your monthly expenses. But first I want to go over some basic Excel terminology so that we're all on the same page. (If you've read *Excel for Beginners* or *Intermediate Excel* you've already seen this so just skip to the end for the discussion on SUMIF/SUMIFS.)

BASIC TERMINOLOGY

Column

Excel uses columns and rows to display information. Columns run across the top of the worksheet and, unless you've done something funky with your settings, are identified using letters of the alphabet. So if I say Column A that's referring to the first column in the worksheet.

Row

Rows run down the side of the worksheet and are numbered starting at 1 and up to a very high number. So if I say Row 1 that's referring to the first row in the worksheet.

Cell

A cell is a combination of a column and row that is identified by the letter of the column it's in and the number of the row it's in. For example, Cell A1 is the cell in the first column and first row of a worksheet.

Spreadsheet

I'll try to avoid using this term, but if I do use it, I'll mean your entire Excel file. It's a little confusing because it can sometimes also be used to mean a specific worksheet, which is why I'll try to avoid it as much as possible.

Worksheet

This is the term I'll use instead. A worksheet is a combination of rows and columns that you can enter data in. When you open an Excel file, it opens to worksheet one. (This is opposed to a workbook which is the entire Excel file that is a collection of one or more worksheets.)

Cell Notation

Formulas in Excel require the use of what I call cell notation. For example, A1:A25 means Cells A1 through A25. If you ever don't understand exactly what a cell range is referencing, type it into Excel using the = sign and see what cells Excel highlights. So, =A1:A25 should highlight cells A1 through A25 and =A1:B25 should highlight the cells in columns A and B and rows 1 through 25.

SUMIF/SUMIFS

This guide uses the SUMIFS formula which is available in versions of Excel starting with Excel 2013. The formula sums values if multiple criteria are met. Prior to 2013 you could use SUMIF to sum values when a single criteria was met but not multiple criteria.

What's important to remember about the SUMIF and SUMIFS formulas is that when using text-based criteria the match has to be exact. (At least the way the formulas used in this guide are written.) So if the formula says to sum all values where the category is "Groceries" then all of your entries that are being summed need to use the category of "Groceries". You can't have "Groceries/Food" or "Food" or "Groceries " with an extra couple of spaces in there. It has to be an exact match for the formula to work.

PAYMENT TRACKING
OVERVIEW

Okay. Now that we've talked about what we're going to do and covered some basic Excel terminology, let's start building our first worksheet, which is going to be a payment tracker.

Here's what it looks like:

	A	B	C	D	E	F	G	H	I
1	Expenses		May			June			July
2	Mortgage	USD	1000	X	USD	1000		USD	1000
3	Electricity*	USD	85	X	USD	100		USD	100
4	Credit Card	USD	455	X	USD	300		USD	300
5	Student Loan*	USD	100		USD	100		USD	100
6	Cable*	USD	100		USD	100		USD	100
7	Internet*	USD	100		USD	100		USD	100
8	Water	USD	100		USD	100		USD	100
9	Garbage	USD	100		USD	100		USD	100
10	Car Insurance*	USD	100		USD	100		USD	100
11	Car Payment*	USD	300		USD	300		USD	300
12	Phone*	USD	100		USD	100		USD	100
13	Gas	CC	100		CC	100		CC	100
14	Misc	CC	100		CC	100		CC	100
15	Groceries	CC	100		CC	100		CC	100
16									
17	Expected Monthly Payments	USD	2540		USD	2400		USD	2400
18	Expected Monthly Credit Card	CC	300		CC	300		CC	300
19									
20	Monthly Payments Remaining	USD	1000		USD	2400		USD	2400
21									

It's a very simple listing for the next three months of all of the bills you need to pay for the month, the amount of those bills, and whether or not those bills have been scheduled to be paid and have in fact been paid.

The first column is a listing of all of your expenses for the month. So mortgage, utilities, student loans, credit cards, etc.

You'll notice that the listing starts with entries that are colored blue and then is followed by entries that are colored brown. The difference between the two colors is that the blue entries are the ones that actually need to be paid this month. The brown entries are what will be charged to a credit card this month and paid next month when that card balance is paid off.

So the brown entries are not counted when we total up the amount due for the month. But it's important to include them to see if your actual spending is in line with what you think you're spending. In my case, I pay off my credit card each month so I can simply compare the values in the brown cells to my credit card bill for the next month. If that's not the case for you, you should compare the total from the brown cells with the total new charges added to your card for that month.

Often it's these discretionary expenses that are the ones that trip people up and cause them to spend too much, so you absolutely need to be tracking them. If you have enough income to cover them, then adjust your expected values. If you don't, this is a place to cut back.

I list my entries in order from earliest due date to latest due date. So in our example above, the mortgage payment is listed first because it's due on the first of the month. Health insurance is listed last because it's due on the 30th of the month.

By listing bills in order of when they're paid you'll be able to quickly scan the list and see where a payment hasn't been made that should have been.

(I also put a small asterisk next to the name for each of the bills that are on autopay so I'll know that they don't need to be scheduled by me and that all I need to do is monitor to make sure the auto-pay occurred when it should have.)

After that first column you'll see that there are three columns of information for each month.

The first monthly column specifies what currency a payment is made in or that the expense is charged. In the sample that's shown with USD, for U.S. Dollars, and CC, for credit card. These letters are then used down at the bottom of the column to help sum the values separately for charged expenses versus paid expenses. (Meaning if you choose not to use them you'll need to also adjust the SUMIFS formulas in Columns C, F, and I.)

For those of you who have expenses in more than one currency, you can also use this column to track your expenses separately for each currency. For example, I split time between the U.S. and New Zealand for a couple of years. When I was doing that I had bills that were due each month in each country and it was important to know how much

I owed in each currency so I could be sure to have the right amount of money available in the right country when it was needed. In that case, I had some entries that used NZD (for New Zealand Dollars) as well as my entries that used USD.

Here's a sample of what that looks like:

	A	B	C	D	E	F	G	H	I
1	Expenses		May			June			July
2	Mortgage US	USD	100	X	USD	100		USD	100
3	Rent NZ	NZD	100		NZD	100		NZD	100
4	Electricity*	USD	100		USD	100		USD	100
5	Credit Card	USD	400		USD	400		USD	400
6	Student Loan*	USD	100		USD	100		USD	100
7	Cable*	USD	100		USD	100		USD	100
8	Internet*	USD	100		USD	100		USD	100
9	Water	USD	100		USD	100		USD	100
10	Garbage	USD	100		USD	100		USD	100
11	Utilities NZ	NZD	100		NZD	100		NZD	100
12	Insurance (Car)*	USD	100		USD	100		USD	100
13	US Phone*	USD	100		USD	100		USD	100
14	NZ Phone	NZD	100		NZD	100		NZD	100
15	Insurance (Health)	USD	100		USD	100		USD	100
16	Gas	CC	100		CC	100		CC	100
17	Misc	CC	100		CC	100		CC	100
18	Travel	CC	100		CC	100		CC	100
19	Groceries	CC	100		CC	100		CC	100
20									
21	Expected Monthly Payments	USD	1400		USD	1400		USD	1400
22		NZD	300		NZD	300		NZD	300
23	Expected Monthly Credit Card	CC	400		CC	400		CC	400
24									
25	Monthly Payments Remaining	USD	1300		USD	1400		USD	1400
26		NZD	300		NZD	300		NZD	300

Going back to the single currency tracker, note that in Columns B, E, and H some of the entries are colored a light gray. This is to show that the payment in question has already been scheduled. So all of the auto-pay entries should be colored gray every month at the beginning of the month and then as you schedule the others you can color those gray as well. This gives a quick visual confirmation that you've scheduled all your payments that need to be scheduled for the month.

When I check this tracker on the 2nd or 3rd of the month I want to see that the first half of my monthly payments are colored gray already since that usually takes me through the 15th of the month. By the 15th I want the rest colored in.

The second column for each month (Columns C, F, and I) lists the month in the top row and then the amount owed for each bill or the expected amount that will be charged to a credit card for that category for that period. When you first populate these values they should be estimated values, but as you receive your bills and know the exact amounts to be paid you should update the values to reflect what you'll actually have to pay. (I usually round up to the nearest five dollars just so I don't have to have $122.31 as an entry. I'll just list that as $125 instead.)

So, for example you'll see in the sample I've provided that for May electricity is listed as $85 but that for June and July it's listed as $100. This is because the estimate for utilities was $100 per month but in that particular month the actual bill was instead something like $83.52.

(It's always a good idea when using estimates of expenses to over-estimate the expense rather than under-estimate because it's better to have a little extra in your pocket than find yourself unexpectedly short of money.)

The third column for each month (Columns D, G, and J) is where you track when a bill has actually been paid. I place an X in the spot next to each bill as it's paid. You can use whatever letter or symbol you want. (The SUMIFS formula we're going to use just looks to see if the cell is blank or not.)

At the bottom of the middle column for each month (Columns C, F, and I), there are three summation formulas.

The first formula is for Expected Monthly Payments. This is the sum of everything you're going to pay that month. So it does not include the CC entries, since those are being charged to a credit card and will be paid the next month.

The second formula is the Expected Monthly Credit Card expense. This is how much you intend to charge for this month. Ideally, it should also be how much you will pay towards your credit card next month so that you're not carrying a balance on that card.

I use the Expected Monthly Credit Card value to compare my expectations against my actual spending. If there's a significant gap, and it can't be explained by something unexpected like needing a new transmission, I know I have an issue I need to address.

(Also, if there's always something unexpected happening to throw off these numbers each month, even if you know what it is, you should start budgeting for that. That's what I use the Misc category for. That's friend's birthdays, oil changes, etc. that consistently occur but aren't always the same thing. It's also my book-buying habit.)

The third formula is for Monthly Payments Remaining. This is how much you still need to pay towards your bills for the month. It's the sum of all the USD values for the month that don't have an X next to them yet.

For later months it's the actual amount you can expect to have to pay for that month and will match your Expected Monthly Payments.

Okay, then. Now that you understand what you're seeing, let's build the sample.

PAYMENT TRACKING
BUILD

This is what we're going to build:

	A	B	C	D	E	F	G	H	I
1	**Expenses**		**May**			**June**			**July**
2	Mortgage	USD	1000	X	USD	1000		USD	1000
3	Electricity*	USD	85	X	USD	100		USD	100
4	Credit Card	USD	455	X	USD	300		USD	300
5	Student Loan*	USD	100		USD	100		USD	100
6	Cable*	USD	100		USD	100		USD	100
7	Internet*	USD	100		USD	100		USD	100
8	Water	USD	100		USD	100		USD	100
9	Garbage	USD	100		USD	100		USD	100
10	Car Insurance*	USD	100		USD	100		USD	100
11	Car Payment*	USD	300		USD	300		USD	300
12	Phone*	USD	100		USD	100		USD	100
13	Gas	CC	100		CC	100		CC	100
14	Misc	CC	100		CC	100		CC	100
15	Groceries	CC	100		CC	100		CC	100
16									
17	Expected Monthly Payments	USD	2540		USD	2400		USD	2400
18	Expected Monthly Credit Card	CC	300		CC	300		CC	300
19									
20	Monthly Payments Remaining	USD	1000		USD	2400		USD	2400

Here we go:

1. In Cell A1 type "Expenses".

2. In Cells C1, F1, and I1 enter your next three months. In this case, "May", "June", and "July".

a. You don't need the quotes when you make your entry. Those are just there to distinguish what to enter.

3. Bold the values in Row 1.

4. In Cells A2 through A15 enter the bills or payables that you want to track and add an asterisk to each one that is on auto-pay. In this case we enter: "Mortgage", "Electricity*", "Credit Card", "Student Loan*", "Cable*", "Internet*", "Water", "Garbage", "Car Insurance*", "Car Payment*", "Phone*", "Gas", "Misc", and "Groceries".

a. As noted above, these should ideally be in chronological order with the bills that are due earlier in the month listed first and the bills that are due at the end of the month listed last.

b. The very bottom entries should be for those categories where you plan to charge the amount rather than pay it directly.

c. If you use cash to pay your expenses, then you'll probably want to have a separate category for that.

5. Color the entries in Column A that you're going to pay each month blue using fill color. In this example that's Cells A2 through A12.

6. Color the entries that you're going to charge each month brown using fill color. In this example that's Cells A13 through A15.

7. In Column B enter USD for bills that will be paid and CC for expenses that will be charged. In this example, USD is used for Cells B2 through B12. CC is used for Cells B13 through B15.

a. If you are not dealing in U.S. Dollars then you'll want to use your own currency abbreviation. For example, EUR for Euros.

8. Color the values in Column B gray using fill color if the bill is on autopay. In this example, that's Cells B3, B5 through B7, and B10 through B12.

9. In Column C add your estimated value for each bill. (See Column F in the sample image for the values to use. Do not use Column C since those are actual values and we'll account for them at the end.)

10. At the end of your range of values in Column C skip one line and calculate your expected monthly payments by taking the sum of all of the USD entries.

a. In this case, the formula is:
=SUMIFS(C2:C15,B2:B15,"USD")

b. If you have an older version of Excel, you could use SUMIF, but you'd need to have the entries in a different order. It would be
=SUMIF(B2:B15,"USD",C2:C15)

11. In Column A of that same row add the text "Expected Monthly Payments".

12. In the next row in Column A add the text "Expected Monthly Credit Card".

13. Go to Column C of that same row, in this case Row 18, and add a formula to sum the values for any credit card payments.

    a. In this case, =SUMIFS(C2:C15,B2:B15,"CC")

    b. If you have an older version of Excel, you could use SUMIF. That formula would be: =SUMIF(B2:B15,"CC",C2:C15)

14. Skip a row and in Column C calculate the value of any payments remaining for that month using SUMIFS to sum all values in Column C where the corresponding value in Column B is USD and the corresponding cell in Column D is blank.

    a. In this example, that would be =SUMIFS(C2:C15,B2:B15,"USD",D2:D15,"")

15. In Column A of that row add the text "Monthly Payments Remaining".

16. In Column B, for each of the calculations add USD or CC to the corresponding cell. So Cells B17 and B20 should be "USD" and Cell B18 should be "CC".

17. Copy Columns B, C, and D and paste into Columns E, F, G and then H, I, J.

18. Go back to the entries for the current month in Column C and change the estimated values to actual values. In this case, in Cells C3 and C4. In Column D mark any bills that have already been paid with an X. In this case, Cells D2 through D4. Shade any cells that are not on auto-pay but have already been scheduled to be paid with gray. In this case Cells B1 and B4.

And that's it. That's your payment tracker. You'll want to customize the entries for your own personal circumstances. If you're dealing with multiple currencies, just add one more row for expected monthly payments and one more for monthly payments remaining and then write the formulas the same except substitute the second currency in for USD.

    And if you pay a lot of expenses in cash then you'll want to use a third fill color for those expenses and track that at the bottom just like you do the Expected Monthly Credit Card except adjusting the formula to add Cash entries instead of CC entries. You'll also need to makes sure you know how much cash you start the month with, how much you withdraw, and then how much you end with so that you can compare your expected cash spending to your actual cash spending. (And, honestly, I don't recommend spending cash because it's too easy to do, but I know some people do that because it's even easier for them to charge uncontrollably on a credit card, so you have to figure out what works best for you and then track it.)

Now let's talk about a simple way to track your cash and credit card spending for a month.

SPEND TRACKING
OVERVIEW

The last tracker looked at what bills you need to pay each month and also had an estimate of how much you think you're going to charge for the month. But it doesn't matter what you think you're going to charge each month if what you actually charge is vastly different from that number. So you need a way to examine what you're actually charging and to assign those charges to categories so you can see where your spending isn't in line with expectations.

Now, there are tools out there that will do this kind of thing for you, like phone apps and some credit card companies even offer a category breakdown of your charges (which are seldom that helpful), but I'm going to also show you a way to do this quite simply using Excel.

The most challenging thing will just be remembering to keep receipts or notes about the money you spend so you can transfer it into your Excel worksheet and then actually doing so. (Which is why I don't actually do this myself on a regular basis.)

So here's what the tracking portion of the tracker looks like:

	A	B	C	D	E
1	Date	Category	Amount	CC/Cash	Notes
2	1-May	Gas	$ 35.42	CC	
3	3-May	Groceries	$ 94.21	CC	
4	4-May	Misc	$ 3.45	Cash	Starbucks
5	6-May	Misc	$ 4.25	Cash	Lunch - Potbelly
6	10-May	Misc	$ 5.32	Cash	Lunch - Chipotle
7	11-May	Gas	$ 24.31	CC	
8					

The first column lists the date of the expense.

The next column lists the category for that expense. (The categories you use here should match what you use in your payment tracker so that you can compare them. If you use more categories here than you use in the payment tracker, it's going to make it more difficult to see whether or not your budgeted amounts match your actual amounts.)

The third column lists how much you spent.

The fourth column lists whether that was done using a credit card or cash.

The fifth column allows you to provide more granular detail. You can put anything you want here, but it's best to use consistent terms throughout a month. So if one of your expenses is Starbucks, always write it that way. Don't do "Starbucks Venti Chai" and "Starbucks Latte" and "Starbucks Muffin and Coffee". That'll make it harder to see patterns in your spending.

If you do end up using a variety of descriptions like I have in the sample with lunch, you can always filter your entries using a text filter, but you'll have to at least have some idea what to filter by. If you don't know that all of your extra spending is happening at Starbucks, you won't know to filter by that.

So I would say that if you really do need that extra level of detail then you should add a column for location and then use the notes column to provide further details.

Listing your spending is literally that simple. Keep your receipts, type the information in, and there you have it.

But there's a second component to this worksheet, which is the summary table. This takes all of those entries in Columns A through E and summarizes your spending by category and by cash or credit in a separate table that I've placed in Columns I through K.

That summary table looks like this:

	H	I	J	K	L
1		Cash	Category	CC	
2		$0.00	Gas	$59.73	
3		$13.02	Misc	$0.00	
4		$0.00	Groceries	$94.21	
5		$13.02	TOTAL	$153.94	
6					

You can then use the totals from the table to compare to your estimated spend amounts that are listed in the payment tracker to see where you're spending more (or less) than you'd anticipated.

Now that you've seen what it does, let's build it.

SPEND TRACKING
BUILD

Once more, this is the first portion of what we're going to build:

	A	B	C	D	E
1	**Date**	**Category**	**Amount**	**CC/Cash**	**Notes**
2	1-May	Gas	$ 35.42	CC	
3	3-May	Groceries	$ 94.21	CC	
4	4-May	Misc	$ 3.45	Cash	Starbucks
5	6-May	Misc	$ 4.25	Cash	Lunch - Potbelly
6	10-May	Misc	$ 5.32	Cash	Lunch - Chipotle
7	11-May	Gas	$ 24.31	CC	
8					

To build it:

1. In Row 1, Cells A1 through E1, add the tracking labels. In this case, "Date", "Category", "Amount", "CC/Cash", and "Notes".

2. Bold Row 1.

3. Format Column A as a date.

4. Format Column C as currency.

5. Add the sample data from the screenshot to Cells A2 through E7.

That's it. It's done. See how simple it is? Now let's build the analysis table.

As a reminder, it looks like this:

	H	I	J	K	
1		Cash	Category	CC	
2		$0.00	Gas	$59.73	
3		$13.02	Misc	$0.00	
4		$0.00	Groceries	$94.21	
5		$13.02	TOTAL	$153.94	
6					

To build it:

1. In Row 1, Cells I1 through K1, add the labels for the summary table. In this case those are "Cash", "Category", and "CC".

2. In Column J, starting with Cell J2 list your categories. In this case, "Gas", "Misc", and "Groceries".

3. In Cell J5, add the label "TOTAL".

4. Bold Column J as well as the total row in the table. In this case, Cells I5, J5, and K5.

5. Format Columns I and K as currency.

6. Use All Borders to place borders around the table and the cells in the table. (So select Cells I1 through K5 and then choose All Borders from the border dropdown menu.)

7. Add blue fill color to the cells in Row 1 of the table in Columns I, J, and K as well as to the TOTAL field. So Cells I1, J1, K1, and J5.

8. Add green fill color to the category labels in Column J. So Cells J2, J3, and J4.

9. In Cell I2 add a SUMIFS formula that totals the values in Columns C when the category matches that in Cell J2 and the payment type listed in Column D is "Cash".

   a. In order to make the formula easy to copy, reference all of Columns C and D rather than a cell range, use $ signs to fix the column and cell references, and use a cell reference to identify the category in Cell J2.

   b. In this case, the formula we're using is:
   =SUMIFS($C:$C,$D:$D,"Cash",$B:$B,$J2)

10. Copy the formula from Cell I2 to the rest of the category rows in Column I. In this case, that would be Cells I3 and I4.

11. Copy the formula from Cell I2 to Cell K2 and change it so that it references CC instead of Cash.

    a. The formula should now be: =SUMIFS($C:$C,$D:$D,"CC",$B:$B,$J2)

12. Copy the formula from K2 down the rest of the categories in the table in Column K. In this case, that would be to Cells K3 and K4.

13. In the total row for Column I, add a formula to sum the individual values for each category where the expense was paid with cash.

    a. In this case that would be in Cell I5 and the formula would be =SUM(I2:I4)

14. Do the same in Column K for expenses that were paid with a credit card.

    a. In this case that would mean adding the formula =SUM(K2:K4) to Cell K5.

————————————————

And that's it. Now you have a worksheet where you can track all of your monthly credit card and cash spending and total the values by category to compare to what you thought you were going to spend in each category. (Not an exercise for the faint of heart, but a necessity if you're going to get your spending under control.)

If you have more categories than the three listed here in the sample, just expand the table to incorporate them by adding additional rows above the total line. The easiest way to do this would be to copy Cells I4 to K4, select in Columns I through K just below that how many new rows you need, right-click and choose Insert Copied Cells, and then choose to Shift Cells Down. You'll now have however many rows of calculations for the Groceries category. Change the category name for each row in Column J and that should be all you have to do as long as the Categories you list in Column J match the categories used in Column B.

Next let's look at money that's readily available to you, which is what I'm calling your current liquid assets. And then we're going to use that to create a simple projection of what things look like over the next three months.

CURRENT LIQUID ASSETS
OVERVIEW

In the next few sections we're going to build a worksheet that has five separate sections, but we're going to break it down into discrete portions rather than try to build the whole thing in one go. This is what it will ultimately look like.(See CURRENT STATUS FINISHING TOUCHES for a larger version):

#	A	B	C	D	E	F	G	H	I	J	K	L	M
1	Date Balance Checked	5/5/2018		Min Bal Req on Accnt		Date Checked	Assets	Value	Liq Value		Assets - Short Term	Liq Value	
2	Personal Checking	$1,500.00		$2,500		4/1/2018	401(k)	$75,000.00	$37,500.00		Cash/Cash Eq	$3,500.00	
3	Personal Savings	$2,000.00		$1,000		5/5/2018	Bank Accounts	$3,500.00	$3,500.00			$3,500.00	
4						5/5/2018	House	$342,500.00	$315,100.00				
5						5/5/2018	Things	$5,000.00	$5,000.00		Assets - Long Term		
6		$3,500.00									Property	$320,100.00	
7								$426,000.00	$361,100.00		Retirement	$37,500.00	
												$357,600.00	
8	May Bills	$1,000.00		Need Monthly									
9	Reserve	$3,500.00		$2,400			Liabilities	Balance	Interest Rate				
10	Income	$3,000.00				5/1/2018	Student Loans	$15,000.00	5% variable		TOTAL ASSETS	$361,100.00	
11				Mos. Covered		5/1/2018	Credit Card	$3,500.00	16.99% variable				
12	Balance at Month End	$2,000.00		0.83		5/1/2018	Mortgage	$328,150.00	4.5% fixed		Liabilities - Short Term		
13											Current Month Bills	$1,000.00	
14	June Bills	$2,400.00						$346,650.00					
15	Income	$3,000.00										$1,000.00	
16				Mos. Covered			Net Worth	$79,350.00			Liabilities - Long Term		
17	Balance at Month End	$2,600.00		1.08			Liq NW	$14,450.00			Credit Card	$3,500.00	
18											Student Loan	$15,000.00	
19	July Bills	$2,400.00				Available Credit					Mortgage	$328,150.00	
20	Income	$3,000.00					Interest Rate	Credit Limit	Available			$346,650.00	
21				Mos. Covered		Credit Card 1	16.99% variable	$10,000.00	$6,500.00				
22	Balance at Month End	$3,200.00		1.33		Line of Credit	9.99% fixed	$3,000.00	$3,000.00		TOTAL LIABILITIES	$347,650.00	
23						Credit Card 2	24.99% variable	$5,000.00	$5,000.00				
24											Short-Term LNW	$2,500.00	
25							Total	$18,000.00	$14,500.00		Long-Term LNW	$10,950.00	
26											LNW	$13,450.00	
27													

As with the rest of what we're doing here, you should ultimately customize this to reflect your own information. But with this section and the next few, I would recommend that you not do so until you have the template built. That's because adding your own information will change the cell references that I'm going to use in the next few sections and may make it more confusing to build the other sections.

(Again, if Excel is easy for you and what we're doing makes sense, then go ahead. But for someone who thinks they might struggle, I'd recommend waiting until the finishing touches section to change the sample to show your personal data.)

Okay?

So the first of these sections, the one in the top left corner, is the list of your current liquid assets. For me that's my checking and savings accounts, because I can access the money in those accounts immediately and without penalty.

If you keep a significant amount of cash on hand you may want to include that as well. Do not include here, however, any accounts you have, like CDs, where you'd have to pay a penalty to access the money today. If you can't transfer it into your checking account and use it to cover that bill that's due tomorrow, it doesn't count. Not for this. (We'll track all assets in a separate section of the worksheet.)

Here's what that portion of the worksheet looks like:

	A	B	C	D
1	Date Balance Checked	5/5/2018		Min Bal Req on Accnt
2	Personal Checking	$1,500.00		$2,500
3	Personal Savings	$2,000.00		$1,000
4				
5				
6		$3,500.00		

In Cell B1 we have the last date your balances were updated. In Cell A1 is the label for that.

Below that we have each account named in Column A and its balance listed in Column B. In this example we have two accounts, a personal checking and a personal savings account.

In my own personal tracker I also have lines for my business checking and savings accounts because I'm a sole proprietor and there are no restrictions on my moving that money into my personal accounts. If you're also self-employed, depending on the type of company you run, this might not be appropriate.

In Column D for each account I've noted the required minimum balance for the account. Many checking and savings accounts will waive your monthly account fee as long as you keep the balance above a certain level. If that matters to you, then you'll want to track what that minimum balance is so that you know when you've gone below it.

In this example, I've used those minimum balances to apply conditional formatting to the values in Column B based on the values in Column D so that I can visually see when an account is below its minimum. If you look at the example you'll see that this is currently the case with the personal checking account listed. The minimum is $2,500 but the account only has $1,500 in it right now so that cell is colored red.

Current Liquid Assets

At the very bottom of the section in Column B there's an entry that sums the total in all of the accounts. In this case that's in Cell B6 and the total is $3,500.

Alright? Makes sense? Let's build it.

CURRENT LIQUID ASSETS
BUILD

Again, this is what we're building:

	A	B	C	D
1	**Date Balance Checked**	5/5/2018		**Min Bal Req on Accnt**
2	**Personal Checking**	$1,500.00		$2,500
3	**Personal Savings**	$2,000.00		$1,000
4				
5				
6		$3,500.00		

To do so:

1. In Cell A1 enter the text "Date Balance Checked" and in Cells A2 and A3 enter the names for the accounts we're tracking, "Personal Checking" and "Personal Savings."

2. Bold those cells.

3. Format Cell B1 as a date and then enter the date.

4. Format Cells B2 through D6 as currency.

5. Enter the balances for the two accounts in Cells B2 and B3. In this case, "$1,500" and "$2,000".

6. In Cell B6 add a formula to sum the balances in the accounts. In this case, =SUM(B2:B5)

7. In Cell D1 add the text "Min Bal Req on Accnt" and bold it.

8. In Cells D2 and D3 add the minimum balances for the two listed accounts. In this case, "$2,500" and "$1,000" respectively.

9. Apply conditional formatting to Cell B2 using a Less Than Highlight Cells rule to color the cell red if the value in B2 is ever less than the value in D2.

   a. For recent versions of Excel go to the Conditional Formatting dropdown in the Home tab, choose Highlight Cells Rules, and then choose Less Than.

10. Do the same for Cell B3 based upon the value in Cell D3.

That's it. That's how you track the total amount available in your liquid accounts, which is usually your checking and savings, and that's how you set a rule so that you know when those accounts fall below their minimum required balances. Now let's take that total balance we just calculated and look at the next three months of incoming and outgoing money.

THREE MONTH PROJECTION
OVERVIEW

The next section of the worksheet gives a quick overview of the next three months. In an ideal world, you'd already have enough money available to cover the next three months' worth of expenses. But the world is not ideal. What I at least aim for is to have what I need for the next month available at the beginning of the month so that no matter what else happens that month my bills are going to be paid. It gives me thirty days to fix things if something goes wrong.

How I track that is using something that looks like this:

	A	B	C	D
6		$3,500.00		
7				
8	May Bills	$1,000.00		Need Monthly
9	Reserve	$3,500.00		$2,400
10	Income	$3,000.00		
11				Mos. Covered
12	Balance at Month End	$2,000.00		0.83
13				
14	June Bills	$2,400.00		
15	Income	$3,000.00		
16				Mos. Covered
17	Balance at Month End	$2,600.00		1.08
18				
19	July Bills	$2,400.00		
20	Income	$3,000.00		
21				Mos. Covered
22	Balance at Month End	$3,200.00		1.33

What you have here is money that you're going to receive and money that you're going to pay out for each of the next three months. And if you look at the very top there you'll see that this continues on from the liquid asset summary we just did. We're going to incorporate that $3,500 into our calculations.

Let's walk through this a little more closely before we build it.

The very top line is the total from the liquid asset section. We then have a gray divider line. And then we start with the current month.

That's the first three lines in Columns A and B. In Cell B8 we have what is still owed for this month's bills. This comes from the Monthly Payments Remaining value in the Payment Tracker for the current month. (Cell C20 from our sample.)

Below that in Cell B9 is the amount you have to keep in reserve in your banking and checking accounts to stay above the minimum balance requirements. This is the sum of the values in Column D of the Current Liquid Assets tracking we just did.

Finally, we have how much money we expect to receive this month. Generally this will be your income, but if you had some other big payout coming this month you could include it here. A student loan disbursement, for example. Or an alimony payment. That kind of thing. Basically, if it's not accounted for in your liquid assets yet, but will be in one of those accounts by the end of the month, you list it here.

Below that we calculate what you'll have at the end of the month. We do this by taking the current liquid assets you have, subtracting the amount you still owe for the month as well as any amounts you need to keep in reserve, and then adding any money you expect to receive.

This gives you where you'll be at the start of next month.

And then below that we do the same thing, without the need to account for the reserve, for the next two months. So in those cases it's just incoming and outgoing.

There's one other thing happening here and that's in Column D. In Cell D9 I've listed the amount needed for each month's expenses. This is the value from the Payment Tracker that's found under the Expected Monthly Payments heading for an average month. In this case, we're using $2,400 from Cell F17 of the Payment Tracker.

Below that, for every one of the three months, we have a calculation of how many months' worth of expenses you can cover with what you'll have as of the end of that month. That's in Cells D12, D17, and D22 and is calculated by taking the balance in Column B for each row and dividing it by the value in Cell D9.

You definitely want those values to be positive for all months. If one of them is not then you're in trouble because you're going to be spending more in that month than you'll have. You're not making it through that month let alone three.

I always want the number for each month-end to be 1 or more. In an ideal world it would be 3 or more.

Now, a quick note about this months covered number. It is not a perfect measure. It can look good. You can have more money coming in this month than you still need to pay for the month, and maybe even end the month with three months of expenses covered. But what this number doesn't show you is timing issues that exist within the current month.

If you're going to get paid a large sum on the 30th but all of your bills are due before then and you don't already have enough on hand to cover those bills, you are in trouble this month even if that is a positive number or a large number. Because you won't have the money when it's needed.

This number does not show intra-month timing issues. It's why I always like to have the current month's expenses already covered on the first of the month. Because then I know I won't have a timing issue like having bills due on the 15th and getting paid on the 16th.

Okay. Now that you know what it does, let's build it.

THREE MONTH PROJECTION
BUILD

Once more, this is what we're going to build:

	A	B	C	D
6		$3,500.00		
7				
8	May Bills	$1,000.00		Need Monthly
9	Reserve	$3,500.00		$2,400
10	Income	$3,000.00		
11				Mos. Covered
12	Balance at Month End	$2,000.00		0.83
13				
14	June Bills	$2,400.00		
15	Income	$3,000.00		
16				Mos. Covered
17	Balance at Month End	$2,600.00		1.08
18				
19	July Bills	$2,400.00		
20	Income	$3,000.00		
21				Mos. Covered
22	Balance at Month End	$3,200.00		1.33

We're using the same worksheet that we used for the current liquid asset tracking. This is going to go directly below that. So:

1. In Cells A8, A9, and A10 add the labels for the current month. In this case that's "May Bills", "Reserve", and "Income".

2. In Cell B8 add the remaining amount owed for the current month from the Payment Tracker. In this case, that's $1,000 taken from Cell C20.

3. In Cell B9 add a formula that sums the total amount you need to reserve to cover your minimum balance requirements. In this case that's =SUM(D2:D5). Color the cell gray using fill color.

4. In Cell B10 add the amount of money you expect to receive in the current month. In this case, that's $3,000.

5. In Cell A12, add a label, "Balance at Month End".

6. In Cell B12, add a formula that takes the balance in your accounts, subtracts the required reserve and bills for the month, and adds the amount you're going to receive for the month.

   a. In this case, that's =B6-B8-B9+B10

7. In Cells A14, A15, and A17, add the labels for the next month. In this case, "June Bills", "Income", and "Balance at Month End".

8. In Cell B14 add the bills for the next month that have not yet been paid. This is taken from the Payment Tracker, Monthly Payments Remaining value for the next month. In this case, the value in Cell F20, $2,400.

   a. It may be less than your Expected Monthly Payments value in Row 18 if you've already paid a bill that's due in the next month.

9. In Cell B15 list the amount you expect to receive in the next month. In this case, $3,000.

10. In Cell B17, calculate the amount you'll have at the end of the month by taking the end-of-month balance for the prior month, subtracting your bills, and adding your income.

    a. In this case, =B12-B14+B15

11. Copy the values in Cells A14 through B17 to Cells A19 through B22 and change the values as needed to reflect the third month. In this case, we had to change Cell A19 to "July Bills" but the rest remained the same.

12. In Cell D8, add the label, "Need Monthly".

13. In Cell D9 add the average value from the Payment Tracker for Expected Monthly Expense. In this case, we're using the value in Cell F17, $2,400.

14. In Cell D11 add the label, "Mos. Covered".

15. In Cell D12 add a formula that takes the month-end balance from Cell B12 and divides it by the amount needed for a typical month. In this case that's =B12/ D9

16. Copy Cells D11 and D12 to Cells D16 and D17 and Cells D21 and D22.

17. If needed, format all of the cells with dollar amounts in them as currency and center. Bold all of the fields with text in them.

———————————

And there you have it. A look at the next three months of cash flows so that you can see if you'll have enough money coming in to cover your expenses for the period. Just remember that there can still be in-month timing issues that you need to be careful of if you don't start each month with at least one month of expenses covered.

This is the three month tracker at its simplest.

I have had far more complex versions that I used at various times. For example, when I was splitting time between the U.S. and New Zealand I had to track my checking/savings accounts by currency and then this whole section had to be expanded to have entries for expenses and income in both currencies and to calculate month-end balances in both currencies as well. Because when you're dealing with more than one currency you have not just timing issues to track, but currency conversion issues to track. Doesn't do you much good to have $10,000 in one currency in one country when you need $200 in another currency in a different country.

Also, because I'm self-employed and have to pay quarterly taxes, my version of this tracker usually has an entry for the current month where I have an amount reserved for my quarterly tax payment. (By putting it in the current month even if it's not due this month I avoid the temptation to use that money to cover my day-to-day expenses.)

Okay. So that was current state. What you have liquid and what you're bringing in and paying out over the next couple months.

Now let's move on to the big picture view. This is your assets, your liabilities, your net worth, and your liquid net worth.

ASSETS
OVERVIEW

We're still working through the same worksheet, but the next three sections will all tie together to form a picture of what you own (your assets), what you owe (your liabilities), and what that means for your overall financial status (your net worth and liquid net worth).

We're going to start with your assets. This is not just your bank accounts, but your home, your car, your retirement account, and anything else you own that has enough value to be worth tracking.

And this includes things that you owe money on, like the house or the car, because when we get to the liability side we'll list what you owe for those assets and then when we put it all together we'll figure out whether what you own is worth more than what you owe. Or not.

So this is what we're going to build first:

	F	G	H	I
1	Date Checked	Assets	Value	Liq Value
2	4/1/2018	401(k)	$75,000.00	$37,500.00
3	5/5/2018	Bank Accounts	$3,500.00	$3,500.00
4	5/5/2018	House	$342,500.00	$315,100.00
5	5/5/2018	Things	$5,000.00	$5,000.00
6				
7			$426,000.00	$361,100.00

It's a basic listing of your assets, what their face value is, and what you could get if you had to sell them today.

There are four parts here.

In Column F you'll list the last date you checked each asset's value.

For my bank accounts I update the balances (in the current liquid assets section) at least three or four times a month. For my home or retirement accounts I do it monthly, but you could do quarterly unless there's a reason to track them more closely.

I would not recommend keeping a constant eye on either of those or any stock investment accounts. It's a good way to give yourself stress you don't need. And especially with stocks, buy and hold is generally a better long-term strategy than trying to time the market. So you should buy these things and then work very hard not to pay attention to the swings in the market because over time they usually resolve themselves.

Column G lists what the assets are. You'll see here that I combine the bank accounts as one entry. You could split them out if you want, but for these purposes I've never seen the need to. Also, this lets me just pull the totals and the dates from Column B in the Current Liquid Assets section.

Column H lists the current value of each asset. Some of these are very straight-forward, like your bank account balances or 401(k) balance. You just need to read the current statement. Some are not so clear, like your house value or car value.

I would encourage you to err on the side of caution and use a lower value for those types of assets rather than the most optimistic value you can find.

For example, a while back Zillow was listing a value for my house that was quite generous. Generous enough that I reached out to my mortgage broker to see about a cash-out refinance. Well, when the actual appraisal of the house came back it was $50,000 less than Zillow's value.

I had the same thing happen when I thought about selling my car a few years back. The Kelley Blue Book® value was not even close to what the dealers wanted to offer. Most wanted to offer half as much.

So better to underestimate your assets rather than overestimate them when it comes to things like house and car values that aren't easy to determine without actually trying to sell the asset.

The final column, Column I, is the one that matters the most and is the hardest to determine. And that's the liquidation value of your assets.

I talk about this in detail in *Budgeting for Beginners*, but I'll give a brief recap here. In this column we're basically saying, "Sure your house is worth $300,000, but that's not what you're going to get if you sell it. You have to pay 6% in broker fees plus all the other little miscellaneous crud like getting a storage unit to hide your clutter and spending a few bucks on getting the house ready. So what you're really going to get if you sell your house tomorrow is about 92% of its value."

For some of your assets, the liquidated value may in fact be zero. If you have a retirement account with your current employer and you aren't vested yet or aren't allowed to borrow against the balance, then it doesn't matter what that value is on paper, for liquidation purposes that asset is worth nothing to you.

Liquidation value is for when it all goes wrong and you have to sell everything you own to get cash. Ask yourself, what cash could I convert that asset into right now? Today. (Or with a house sale, within two months.) That's what should be in this column. If you started the liquidation process today, what would you get for that asset?

For me, that's 92% of my house value (that I'm conservative in estimating) and 50% of my 401(k) from an old employer where I'd have to pay taxes and a 10% early withdrawal penalty because I'm not retirement age yet.

You'll need to figure that out for your particular circumstances and each of your assets.

Remember to be conservative with this and underestimate rather than overestimate. Better to think you don't have enough money and be wrong than think you have enough and be wrong.

Okay, let's build the sample.

ASSETS

BUILD

Remember that we're still working in the same worksheet that we used for the current liquid assets and three month projection. So we're just going to go back to the top of the worksheet and move over a couple of columns.

Here's what we're building:

	F	G	H	I
1	**Date Checked**	**Assets**	**Value**	**Liq Value**
2	4/1/2018	401(k)	$75,000.00	$37,500.00
3	5/5/2018	Bank Accounts	$3,500.00	$3,500.00
4	5/5/2018	House	$342,500.00	$315,100.00
5	5/5/2018	Things	$5,000.00	$5,000.00
6				
7			$426,000.00	$361,100.00

1. In Row 1, Columns F through I, add your column headings, "Date Checked", "Assets", "Value", and "Liq Value". Bold them.

2. In Column F list the date each balance was last checked. For the Bank Accounts entry, use a formula that pulls in the date from Column B. In this case =B1 in Cell F3.

3. In Column G list your assets. In this case, that's "401(k)", "Bank Accounts", "House", and "Things".

4. In Column H list the current value for each asset. For the Bank Accounts entry, use a formula that pulls that value from Column B. In this case =B6 in Cell H3.

5. In Column I add a formula to calculate your liquidated value for each asset.

   a.   In this case, I2 is =H2*(0.5), I3 is =H3, I4 is =H4*0.92, and I5 is =H5.

6. Skip one row after your last entry and add a summary row to total the current value of your assets as well as their current liquidated value. In this case, that's =SUM(H2:H6) in H7 and =SUM(I2:I6) in I7.

And that's it. The most complex part of this section is figuring out your liquidated values, but that's also key to being able to handle any sort of unexpected financial disruptions. A little bit later we're going to break this liquidated assets value down further by short-term and long-term and that's where you'll really start to see how important cash flow can be.

But for now, time to do the liabilities.

LIABILITIES

OVERVIEW

Assets are only half of the picture. Just as important as what you own is what you owe. So the counterpart to tracking what you own (your assets) is tracking what you owe (your liabilities). Nice thing with liabilities is there's no haircutting involved.

(If you have a debt that has an early payoff penalty you could gross up the amount of the liability by that amount, which would be the equivalent to haircutting your assets, but please tell me you don't have any debts like that. Those things are bad news.)

Okay, here it is. This is what we're going to build.

	F	G	H	I
9		Liabilities	Balance	Interest Rate
10	5/1/2018	Student Loans	$15,000.00	5% variable
11	5/1/2018	Credit Card	$3,500.00	16.99% variable
12	5/1/2018	Mortgage	$328,150.00	4.5% fixed
13				
14			$346,650.00	

It goes directly below the assets listing we just created.

Just like with the assets, the first column, Column F, is the date that you last checked the balance. (The label for this column is in the Assets section.)

The second column, Column G, is a listing of your different types of debt (your liabilities). In the sample we have student loans, credit card, and mortgage. You should have a separate line for each company you owe money. So if you have two credit cards, have a line for each of them. Three student loans, three separate lines.

And you can call them whatever you want, just be sure you know what that liability is. I usually list them by company name. So AES for my student loan, for example.

The third column, Column H, is what you owe on each one. Be sure that this is the correct amount. For example, my student loans will often show one value on the main screen, but have a higher value on a different screen where they include accrued interest for the month. You want the higher balance because that's what you'll have to pay if you pay that debt off.

In the fourth column, Column I, I like to list the interest rate that applies on each one. This helps me quickly prioritize which to pay off when I get some extra money in and want to pay off a debt.

I pay off any debt with a temporary low rate that's about to expire and then either higher interest rate debt or debt with a variable interest rate if interest rates are on the rise.

Also, keep in mind that some debt comes with better "benefits" than other debt. So, for example, student loans can be deferred or you can get a forbearance on them if you are in financial difficulty, whereas that isn't an option with credit card debt.

Finally, below Column H I calculate the total balance for all of my liabilities. In this example, that's in Cell H14.

So that's it. Pretty simple. Let's go build it.

LIABILITIES
BUILD

Here's what the sample looks like:

	F	G	H	I
9		Liabilities	Balance	Interest Rate
10	5/1/2018	Student Loans	$15,000.00	5% variable
11	5/1/2018	Credit Card	$3,500.00	16.99% variable
12	5/1/2018	Mortgage	$328,150.00	4.5% fixed
13				
14			$346,650.00	

To build it:

1. In Cells G9, H9, and I9 add your labels, "Liabilities", "Balance", and "Interest Rate". Bold them.

2. In Cells F10 through I12 add information on your liabilities and their balances. In this case that means:

   a. Adding the date "5/1/2018" to Cells F10 through F12,

   b. Listing "Student Loans", "Credit Cards", and "Mortgage" in Cells G10 through G12,

   c. Listing "$15,000", "$3,500", and $328,150" for balances in Cells H10 through H12, and

   d. Listing rate information, "5% variable", "16.99% variable", and "4.5% fixed" in Cells I10 through I12.

3. In Cell H14 add a formula to calculate the total dollar value of all of the liabilities.

    a. In this case using the formula =SUM(H10:H12)

And that's it. It's just a very basic listing of information on your liabilities. As with the assets section, you'll want to customize this for your own information, which probably means having more rows of information than I'm showing here. Just be sure that the total liabilities calculation updates to include all of the entries.

Now we're going to take the asset and liability information and calculate both a net worth and a liquid net worth

NET WORTH AND LIQUID NET WORTH
OVERVIEW

Once you know what you own (your assets) and what you owe (your liabilities) it's time to put those numbers to work. The most common calculation for this is your net worth. That's your assets minus your liabilities.

Personally, I don't have much use for net worth. It's a pretty number that does nothing for me.

Because if I can't liquidate my assets to pay off my liabilities the value of those assets really doesn't do much for me. It has as much value to me as the piece of paper it's printed on, which is nothing.

What matters to me is my liquid net worth. This is how much I would have if I had to sell off everything I own to pay off everything I owe. If I were starting back at square one, would I be able to do that? Would I have money leftover? Or do I owe more than I own?

That number has significance. And that's the one I always want to be a positive number. (Not always gonna happen, unfortunately. When I was a student that was definitely not the case. I had student debt, credit card debt, and no savings. But as a forty-something adult with a real job, I now expect that number to be positive and if it isn't I'm going to take steps to make sure it is. Which usually means earning more money somehow.)

We'll calculate another measure in a minute—short-term liquid net worth—which is actually the number I live and die by. If that one is negative you have immediate issues you need to fix. But your overall liquid net worth being a negative number is a potential early warning sign of future financial issues.

So let's add the calculation of net worth and liquid net worth to our worksheet.

NET WORTH AND LIQUID NET WORTH BUILD

This one is very simple. We're just adding two calculations to the bottom of our assets and liabilities section. Here's the whole section:

	F	G	H	I
1	Date Checked	Assets	Value	Liq Value
2	4/1/2018	401(k)	$75,000.00	$37,500.00
3	5/5/2018	Bank Accounts	$3,500.00	$3,500.00
4	5/5/2018	House	$342,500.00	$315,100.00
5	5/5/2018	Things	$5,000.00	$5,000.00
6				
7			$426,000.00	$361,100.00
8				
9		Liabilities	Balance	Interest Rate
10	5/1/2018	Student Loans	$15,000.00	5% variable
11	5/1/2018	Credit Card	$3,500.00	16.99% variable
12	5/1/2018	Mortgage	$328,150.00	4.5% fixed
13				
14			$346,650.00	
15				
16		Net Worth	$79,350.00	
17		Liq NW	$14,450.00	

All we need to add are those two lines at the bottom in Cells G16 to H17. So:

1. In Cell G16 and G17 add the labels "Net Worth" and "Liq NW".
2. In Cell H16 add a formula that takes your total assets value and subtracts your total liabilities value.

   a.   In this case that formula is =H7-H14

3.   In Cell H17 add a formula that takes the liquidated value of your assets and subtracts your total liabilities value.

   a.   In this case that formula is =I7-H14

And that's it. You'll notice that we used the same value for the liabilities in both cases, but that the value for the assets was different in each formula because of the difference in the liquidated value. If you did have some strange liability that had a different real-time value, then you'd need to use that balance instead for your liquid net worth calculation.

Next let's look at your available credit. This is basically how much of a safety net you have in place in case things go bad.

AVAILABLE CREDIT
OVERVIEW

Right below assets and liabilities we're going to add a section to track your available credit. As I mentioned above, this is basically a measure of what kind of safety net you have if things go wrong. If all of your credit cards are maxed out and the car needs a new transmission, you're going to be in trouble. But if you have $10,000 available on a credit card, then you'll be able to pay for the car repairs and continue to show up to work every day to earn money to pay that expense off.

Having available credit can be the difference between a few tight months and utter catastrophe. That's why I'm an advocate of always having at least one more credit card or line of credit than you need. (Although I should warn you to keep an eye on this because if you don't use it credit companies sometimes will drop your limit on you without warning. I once had a card go from a $7,500 limit to $500 without any warning it was going to happen.)

Okay. So this is what this portion of the worksheet looks like:

	F	G	H	I
19	**Available Credit**			
20		**Interest Rate**	**Credit Limit**	**Available**
21	Credit Card 1	16.99% variable	$10,000.00	$6,500.00
22	Line of Credit	9.99% fixed	$3,000.00	$3,000.00
23	Credit Card 2	24.99% variable	$5,000.00	$5,000.00
24				
25		Total	$18,000.00	$14,500.00
26				

The first column, Column F, lists your various sources of credit. So any credit cards, overdraft balances, or lines of credit.

The second column, Column G, lists the interest rate for each one. This is important if you need to use one long-term so that you can choose the one that's going to cost you the least amount of money in interest.

The third column, Column H, lists how much money is potentially available to you. So, your credit limit.

The fourth column, Column I, lists how much of that credit limit you still have available. This is a calculation using the amount you've already used as listed in the liabilities section and subtracting that amount from your credit limit in Column H. If you haven't drawn down a particular line of credit, then this will just be the value in the third column.

At the bottom of the entries in Columns H and I are formulas that sum the total of all available credit and the total still available to use.

Okay, then. Let's go build this.

AVAILABLE CREDIT
BUILD

This is what we're building:

	F	G	H	I
19	**Available Credit**			
20		**Interest Rate**	**Credit Limit**	**Available**
21	Credit Card 1	16.99% variable	$10,000.00	$6,500.00
22	Line of Credit	9.99% fixed	$3,000.00	$3,000.00
23	Credit Card 2	24.99% variable	$5,000.00	$5,000.00
24				
25		Total	$18,000.00	$14,500.00
26				

To do so:

1. In Cell F19 add the label "Available Credit" and bold it.

2. In Cells G20, H20, and I20 add the labels, "Interest Rate", "Credit Limit", and "Available" and bold them.

3. In Column F list your available lines of credit. In this case, "Credit Card 1", "Line of Credit", and "Credit Card 2" in Cells F21 through F23.

4. In Column G list the corresponding interest rates for each one. In this case "16.99% variable", "9.99% fixed", and "24.99% variable" in Cells G21 through G23.

5. In Column H list the corresponding credit limit for each one. In this case, "$10,000", "$3,000", and "$5,000" in Cells H21 through H23.

6. In Column I add a formula to calculate the amount of credit still remaining for each account. In Cell I21 that is =I21-I11. In Cell J22 that is =I22. And in Cell J23 that is =I23.

7. At the bottom of the entries add the label "Total". In this case, in Cell G25.

8. Next to that in Column H add a formula to total up your total credit. In this case =SUM(H21:H23) in Cell H25.

9. And next to that in Column I add a formula to total up your remaining available credit. In this case =SUM(I21:I23) in Cell I25.

———

Once more, as you customize this you may have more entries than the three I've listed here. If you heavily use your lines of credit it may make sense to have entries in your liabilities section for each one even when the balance on that line is zero so that you can properly build the formulas in Column I of this section and not have to worry about updating them as you use a new line of credit.

Finally, let's look at the last component for this worksheet which is your short-term and long-term liquid net worth.

SHORT-TERM LIQUID NET WORTH
OVERVIEW

What I call short-term liquid net worth is to me the single-most important number in this entire workbook. Because it's the number that tells you if you can keep going. You could owe a million dollars and it wouldn't matter if that million dollars was due twenty years from now. Sure, twenty years from now it would matter. But until then? No. You could live just fine with that debt hanging over your head.

What matters is that you have enough cash on hand or coming in now to pay what you owe now. If you can find a (legal) way to keep meeting your current obligations then the actual amount of debt you carry is irrelevant.

Now, let me unpack that a little. Because it's not an ideal way to handle your finances. The more debt you carry, the more precarious your situation is overall. Right?

Because if you have $100,000 in debt then chances are you have to make higher monthly payments on that debt than if you have only $10,000 in debt. Also, the interest that's going to accrue on $100,000 is higher than the interest that's going to accrue on $10,000. Meaning that long-term you are probably going to be in far worse shape the more debt you carry.

So having debt isn't "good". But having debt isn't necessarily "bad" either. Heck, that's the only way I was able to go to college, buy my first reliable car, and buy any of the houses I've ever owned. If I'd just had to live with cash-in-hand, I'd have had a much less successful life than I have. No college education means no good job means no good income which means no mortgage loan, etc.

But getting back to the point. Your short-term liquid net worth, which is the amount of cash or cash equivalents that you have minus the amount you owe now or within the next few weeks, is crucial. Because if you can keep that number positive, you can keep going. Let that number go negative and you're looking at bounced checks, creditor calls, and possibly bankruptcy.

Knowing that you have the money to meet your current debts is essential. So here's what we're going to calculate:

	K	L
1	Assets - Short Term	Liq Value
2	Cash/Cash Eq	$3,500.00
3		$3,500.00
4		
5	Assets - Long Term	
6	Property	$320,100.00
7	Retirement	$37,500.00
8		$357,600.00
9		
10	TOTAL ASSETS	$361,100.00
11		
12	Liabilities - Short Term	
13	Current Month Bills	$1,000.00
14		$1,000.00
15		
16	Liabilities - Long Term	
17	Credit Card	$3,500.00
18	Student Loan	$15,000.00
19	Mortgage	$328,150.00
20		$346,650.00
21		
22	TOTAL LIABILITIES	$347,650.00
23		
24	Short-Term LNW	$2,500.00
25	Long-Term LNW	$10,950.00
26	LNW	$13,450.00

It looks complicated, but it's really not.

First, you take the liquidated value of your assets and you classify them as either short-term or long-term. For me, I classify what I have in the bank as short-term as well as any receivable from a reliable customer that's going to pay out in the next month. Everything else, like my house which would take probably two months to sell, I classify as a long-term asset.

Next, we do the same thing with our liabilities. Ask yourself which debts you're going to pay in the next month and which you'll have to pay sometime after that. So here I've taken the current month's remaining expense and listed that as a short-term liability. But because that doesn't show me paying off the credit card balance (which is more than this amount) I've put the credit card balance into the long-term liability category.

On my personal worksheet, because I pay off my credit card every month, I have my credit card listed as a short-term liability. If I hit a point where I am not paying off that card every month, then I will move that to a long-term liability.

So liabilities can and do move. If I were to sell my house, for example, the month I was closing on that sale I could technically move the house liquidation value to short-term assets and the corresponding liability to short-term liabilities.

But in general the categories will stay static once you set them up.

Once you've classified your assets and liabilities as short-term or long-term, then it's just a matter of doing some math. Take your short-term assets and subtract your short-term liabilities. Take your long-term assets and subtract your long-term liabilities.

And remember, short-term liquid net worth is the number that matters the most.

SHORT-TERM LIQUID NET WORTH BUILD

Here's the sample.

	K	L
1	**Assets - Short Term**	**Liq Value**
2	Cash/Cash Eq	$3,500.00
3		**$3,500.00**
4		
5	**Assets - Long Term**	
6	Property	$320,100.00
7	Retirement	$37,500.00
8		**$357,600.00**
9		
10	**TOTAL ASSETS**	**$361,100.00**
11		
12	**Liabilities - Short Term**	
13	Current Month Bills	$1,000.00
14		**$1,000.00**
15		
16	**Liabilities - Long Term**	
17	Credit Card	$3,500.00
18	Student Loan	$15,000.00
19	Mortgage	$328,150.00
20		**$346,650.00**
21		
22	**TOTAL LIABILITIES**	**$347,650.00**
23		
24	**Short-Term LNW**	**$2,500.00**
25	**Long-Term LNW**	**$10,950.00**
26	**LNW**	**$13,450.00**

To build it:

1. In Cells K1 and L1 add the labels, "Assets-Short Term" and "Liq Value" and bold them.

2. Below this in Column K list your short-term assets. In this case, "Cash/Cash Eq" in Cell K2.
   a. If you had cash, you'd include it here as well as any other asset that's going to be converted to cash in the next month or could be.

3. In Column L include a cell reference to where the value for each short term asset is listed in Column I, our assets section. In this case, Cell L2 should be =I3.
   a. By including a cell reference you ensure that the values update as you change your information in the rest of the worksheet.

4. At the end of the current assets listing, include a formula to total the liquid value of your current assets. In this case =SUM(L2) in Cell L3. Bold the value.

5. Skip one line and in Column K add the label, "Assets-Long Term" and bold it. In this case, that's in Cell K5.

6. Below that in Column K list your long-term assets. In this case "Property" and "Retirement" in Cells K6 and K7.

7. In Column L for each asset include a formula that references the value for each in Column I, the assets section.
   a. In this case, for property we've combined things and house together so in Cell L6 we use =I5+I4.
   b. In Cell L7 we use =I2.

8. In the next row in Column L add a formula to total your long-term assets.
   a. In this case that's =SUM(L6:L7)

9. Skip a row and in Column K add the label "TOTAL ASSETS" and bold it. In Cell K10 in this example.

10. Next to that in Column L add a formula to combine your short-term assets and your long-term assets. In this case, =L3+L8 in Cell L10. This amount should match the total liquidated assets value in Column I.

11. Skip a row and in Column K add the label, "Liabilities-Short Term". In this case in Cell K12. Bold it.

12. Starting with the next row list your short-term liabilities in Column K. In this case we list "Current Month Bills" in Cell K13.

13. In Column L list the value for each liability using a cell reference to the liabilities or current month's bills value. In this case, Cell L13 uses =B8.

14. In the next row in Column L add a formula to total all of the short term liabilities. In this case =SUM(L13:L13) in Cell L14.

15. Skip a row and in Column K add the label "Liabilities-Long Term". In this example, that's in Cell K16. Bold the entry.

16. Below that in Column K list each of your long-term liabilities. In this case that's "Credit Card", "Student Loan", and "Mortgage" in Cells K17 through K19.

17. In Column L use cell references to pull in the balances for each liability.

    a. For Cell L17 that's =H11

    b. For Cell L18 that's =H10

    c. For Cell L19 that's =H12

18. On the next line in Column L add a formula to calculate your total long-term liabilities. In this case, =SUM(L17:L19) in Cell L20. Bold it.

19. Skip a row and in Column K add the label "TOTAL LIABILITIES" and bold it. In this case, in Cell K22.

20. In that same row in Column L, add a formula to sum your short-term and your long-term liabilities. In this case, that would be =L14+L20 in Cell L22.

21. Skip a row and then in the next three rows in Column K add the labels "Short-Term LNW", "Long-Term LNW", and "LNW" where LNW stands for liquid net worth. In the example this is in Cells K24 through K26.

22. In Column L for Short-Term LNW take your short-term assets and subtract your short-term liabilities. In the example, this is in Cell L24 and should be =L3-L14.

23. In Column L for Long-Term LNW take your long-term assets and subtract your long-term liabilities. In the example, this is in Cell L25 and should be =L8-L20.

24. In Column L for LNW take your total assets and subtract your total liabilities. In the example, this is in Cell L26 and should be =L10-L22.

    a. Your total liquid net worth should equal your short-term liquid net worth added to your long-term liquid net worth.

If there is a discrepancy between the liquid net worth calculated here and the one calculated in the assets and liabilities section, that's because we've incorporated the current month payable amount. Otherwise, each of the assets and liabilities you had listed in the prior section should be categorized as long or short-term and included here in these calculations.

You may want to or need to include your current month's income in your asset listing in order to have a positive number for your short-term liquid net worth. Only do this if you have already worked those hours or been guaranteed that income, because otherwise that money shouldn't be counted on as an asset because you never know what might happen.

CURRENT STATUS
FINISHING TOUCHES

Okay. That was a lot to put on one worksheet. But the nice thing about doing it this way is that now you have one place to look for a snapshot of how you're doing financially. The left-hand side is the next few months. The middle is the big picture. And the right-hand side tells you if you are facing a cash crisis anytime soon or if your assets and liabilities are out of balance in terms of when they come due.

Before we move on, I just want to do some prettying up by adding gray fill color to separate each of the sections. So we want our final version to look like this:

	A	B	C	D	E	F	G	H	I	J	K	L	M
1	Date Balance Checked	5/5/2018	Min Bal Req on Acnt			Date Checked	Assets	Value	Liq Value		Assets - Short Term	Liq Value	
2	Personal Checking	$1,500.00	$2,500			4/1/2018	401(k)	$75,000.00	$37,500.00		Cash/Cash Eq	$3,500.00	
3	Personal Savings	$2,000.00	$1,000			5/5/2018	Bank Accounts	$3,500.00	$3,500.00			$3,500.00	
4						5/5/2018	House	$342,500.00	$315,100.00		Assets - Long Term		
5						5/5/2018	Things	$5,000.00	$5,000.00		Property	$320,100.00	
6		$3,500.00									Retirement	$37,500.00	
7								$426,000.00	$361,100.00		TOTAL ASSETS	$357,600.00	
8	May Bills			Need Monthly									
9	Reserve	$3,500.00		$2,400		Liabilities		Balance	Interest Rate		Liabilities - Short Term		
10	Income	$3,000.00		Mos. Covered		5/1/2018	Student Loans	$15,000.00	5% variable		Current Month Bills	$1,000.00	
11						5/1/2018	Credit Card	$3,500.00	16.99% variable				
12	Balance at Month End	$2,000.00		0.83		5/1/2018	Mortgage	$328,150.00	4.5% fixed		Liabilities - Short Term	$1,000.00	
13													
14	June Bills	$2,400.00					Net NW	$79,350.00			Liabilities - Long Term		
15	Income	$3,000.00					Liq NW	$14,450.00			Credit Card	$3,500.00	
16				Mos. Covered							Student Loan	$15,000.00	
17	Balance at Month End	$2,600.00		1.08							Mortgage	$328,150.00	
18											TOTAL LIABILITIES	$346,650.00	
19	July Bills	$2,400.00				Available Credit	Interest Rate	Credit Limit	Available		Short-Term LNW	$2,500.00	
20	Income	$3,000.00		Mos. Covered		Credit Card 1	16.99% variable	$10,000.00	$6,500.00		Long-Term LNW	$10,950.00	
21						Line of Credit	9.99% fixed	$3,000.00	$3,000.00		LNW	$13,450.00	
22	Balance at Month End	$3,200.00		1.33		Credit Card 2	24.99% variable	$5,000.00	$5,000.00				
23						Total		$18,000.00	$14,500.00				
24													
25													
26													
27													

Using the sample that I've been building on throughout the last sections, to add the dividers, do the following:

1. Add gray fill color to Cells A7 through D7, Cells F18 through I18, and Cells A27 through M27.
2. Change the width of Column E so that it's about the same as the height of any of the lines in the table. So a height of approximately 2.
3. Add gray fill color to Cells E1 through E27.
4. Use the Format Painter to copy the column width and cell colors from Column E to Columns J and M.

And that's it. You're done with the sample. Now would be the time to go back and personalize all of this with your own data. Just remember that as you insert into certain sections that if you want the gray lines to stay lined up you need to insert cells in that entire section. (If you mess it up, which I do often, just go back into the column that is out of alignment and insert the number of cells you need to get everything lined back up.)

Also, if you think you're going to be printing this document on a regular basis, once it's finalized with your data I would suggest selecting the entire area (in the sample that would be Cells A1 through M27) and then choosing Set Print Area under the Page Layout tab. This document also prints best in Landscape orientation. You may also need to scale the page so that all columns appear on one page.

So that was pretty much all an individual really needs. The next two worksheets we're going to build are for more specialized circumstances. The next one is a simple receivables tracker that I use for self-publishing that lets me track payments due by currency and convert those to U.S. Dollars. So if you're not self-employed or you use software to track these things, you can skip it.

The last worksheet we're going to build is one I find useful for general scenario analysis and I think anyone can benefit from, but it's not directly budget-related. It's a straight-forward way to analyze different possible outcomes when you have two possible variables like house price and broker commission or hourly pay and hours worked per week. Do make sure to check it out if you decide to skip the receivables tracking we're going to do next.

RECEIVABLES TRACKING
OVERVIEW

Now we're going to talk about how to build a receivables tracker. As I just mentioned, this is for the self-employed people like me who don't use some sort of accounting software.

How complex you need your receivables tracker to be will depend very much on what type of work you do.

So, for example, most of the time I was doing regulatory consulting I had one primary client at a time who paid me once a month. In that case, I had a very simple listing of the day I'd billed them, the dates covered by that bill, the amount I'd billed, and the date I expected payment. I then checked those amounts off as I was paid. I also had a tax payable calculation based upon the amount I'd received year-to-date.

With writing, things are a little more complex. I have nine different places where I sell my books or video courses and one of them, Amazon, has at least seven different countries that can issue payments each month. So it's not uncommon for me to have over fifteen different payments each month, all from different sources and some in different currencies.

So for writing I have one set of columns where I track what I've earned each month and a table at the bottom of that set of columns that converts any amounts in foreign currency to an estimated U.S. Dollar amount.

It looks like this:

◢	A	B	C	D	E
1	Money Earned to Be Paid in Current Year				
2					
3	Month	Income	Source	Currency	Paid
4	October 2017	$ 75.00	Vendor 1	USD	X
5	November 2017	$ 125.00	Vendor 2	USD	X
6	November 2017	$ 110.00	Vendor 3	USD	X
7	November 2017	$ 115.00	Vendor 4	USD	X
8	December 2017	$ 215.00	Vendor 1	USD	
9	December 2017	$ 185.00	Vendor 2	CAD	
10	December 2017	$ 115.00	Vendor 3	AUD	
11	December 2017	$ 125.00	Vendor 4	GBP	
12					
13					
14		Total Outstanding			
15		$ 215.00	*USD*	$ 215.00	
16		$ 185.00	*CAD*	$ 147.82	
17		$ 125.00	*GBP*	$ 170.00	
18		$ -	*EUR*	$ -	
19		$ 115.00	*AUD*	$ 89.93	
20		$ -	*INR*	$ -	
21		USD Value		$ 622.75	
22					

And then another set of columns in that same worksheet where I track payments once they're received and calculate a potential tax due on those earnings. (We'll look at that one in a minute.)

With this first one, if you're only dealing in payments in one currency then don't worry about building the table at the bottom of that first image. You won't need it.

So what do we have here?

Columns A through E are for tracking money you've earned that is going to be paid in the current calendar year. (If you have a tax year that's different from the calendar year, then I'd suggest tracking based on tax year instead.)

In this example that's money that will be paid in 2018 even though some of that money was earned in 2017. (This is because I use cash-basis accounting. Meaning I pay taxes when I receive the cash not when I earn it.)

Column A lists the month the money was earned.

Column B lists how much was earned from that source for that month.

(I complete these entries at the beginning of the next month. So for January I'll list values in my tracker on February 2nd or 3rd. For some vendors that means I don't have an actual amount they're going to pay me yet. What I do is use a guesstimate and highlight it in yellow to indicate that it's a temporary value that is subject to change. If you do this, always be sure to err on the side of caution and underestimate what you'll be paid. So, for example, for Amazon page reads I use an estimate of .0042 even though the usual payout is closer to .0045 when it's announced on the 15th of the next month.)

Column C lists the source of the income listed. In the sample we have Vendor 1, Vender 2, etc. But my actual entries are things like Amazon AUS, Amazon UK, ACX, etc.

Column D lists the currency associated with that income. (If you only have earnings in one currency then this column can be eliminated but you'll also need to adjust the SUMIF function at the bottom of the table for calculating outstanding payments.)

Column E is for indicating whether or not a payment has been received yet. Simply place a mark in the corresponding cell in this column to reflect payment. I use an X.

You'll see that below the entries in Columns A through E I also include a table of Total Outstanding payments. If you are only dealing with receivables in one currency, you do not need this whole table. You can simply use a SUMIF function that adds all values in Column B when Column E is blank.

But since I do have multiple currencies to deal with, I create this table to add values by currency and then convert them to my currency.

In Column B of the table is a SUMIFS function for each currency that adds up all outstanding payments in that currency that have not yet been paid.

Column C of the table lists each currency.

(The currency abbreviation you use here should match the abbreviation used in Column D in your payment listings above. So, "USD" has to be in both the table and the detailed entries. You can't have USD in one and U.S. Dollars in the other. I mean you could, it'll just make your life harder because you'll have to customize the formula used for each currency.)

Column D of the table lists each of the values from Column B converted over to my currency, U.S. Dollars. And then at the bottom of the table I have a formula that takes the total value of all outstanding payments in my currency.

Because currency conversion rates move all the time, this is just an estimated value. The actual amount paid won't be known until that payment is finally received.

So that's the first half, receivables due. The other half is the payment tracker.

Here it is:

	G	H	I	J	K
1	Payments Received in Current Year				
2					
3	Date Received	Source	Amount	Tax Liab	For
4	1/2/2018	Vendor 1	$ 75.00	$ 18.75	Vendor 1 October
5	1/9/2018	Vendor 2	$125.00	$ 31.25	Vender 2 November
6	1/16/2018	Vendor 3	$110.00	$ 27.50	Vendor 3 November
7	1/19/2018	Vendor 4	$115.00	$ 28.75	Vendor 4 November
8					
9					
10			$425.00	$106.25	
11					

Column G lists the date the payment was received. (Useful for calculating quarterly tax payments.)

Column H lists the source of the payment. This should be the same as the source in Column C.

Column I lists the amount received in my currency.

Column J calculates a tax due on that value. In this case I'm using 25%. Your effective tax rate may be higher or lower than that but this at least gives a nice quick estimate of taxes owed on this income.

Column K lists what the payment was for. Usually I repeat the vendor name and then list the month of income the payment relates to. You can list whatever you want here, just make sure it lets you track back to your money earned entries.

At the bottom I have a row that calculates total amount received so far this year and total estimated taxes due so far. (On my personal worksheet I then pull that tax due amount over into my liabilities tracking and adjust it for any tax payments I've already made for the year.)

That's it.

One set of columns to track what you've earned, one set of columns to track what you've received. And then, of course, you'll want to monitor this to make sure that you're receiving all of the payments you're due when they're due.

If you wanted to get even more fancy, you could add a column to the money earned set of columns that lists the date you expect payment. And if you wanted to be really really fancy, you could apply conditional formatting to show when a payment is past due. Fortunately, I may not always know what I'm going to get paid but the vendors I deal with at least pay on time.

Alright. Let's build this.

RECEIVABLES TRACKING
BUILD

As a reminder, here is what we're building:

	A	B	C	D	E	F	G	H	I	J	K
1	Money Earned to Be Paid in Current Year						Payments Received in Current Year				
2											
3	Month	Income	Source	Currency	Paid		Date Received	Source	Amount	Tax Liab	For
4	October 2017	$ 75.00	Vendor 1	USD	X		1/2/2018	Vendor 1	$ 75.00	$ 18.75	Vendor 1 October
5	November 2017	$ 125.00	Vendor 2	USD	X		1/9/2018	Vendor 2	$ 125.00	$ 31.25	Vender 2 November
6	November 2017	$ 110.00	Vendor 3	USD	X		1/16/2018	Vendor 3	$ 110.00	$ 27.50	Vendor 3 November
7	November 2017	$ 115.00	Vendor 4	USD	X		1/19/2018	Vendor 4	$ 115.00	$ 28.75	Vendor 4 November
8	December 2017	$ 215.00	Vendor 1	USD							
9	December 2017	$ 185.00	Vendor 2	CAD							
10	December 2017	$ 115.00	Vendor 3	AUD					$425.00	$106.25	
11	December 2017	$ 125.00	Vendor 4	GBP							
12											
13											
14			Total Outstanding								
15		$ 215.00	USD	$ 215.00							
16		$ 185.00	CAD	$ 147.82							
17		$ 125.00	GBP	$ 170.00							
18		$ -	EUR	$ -							
19		$ 115.00	AUD	$ 89.93							
20		$ -	INR	$ -							
21			USD Value	$ 622.75							
22											

So:

1. In Cell A1 and in Cell G1 add the labels for the two sections, "Money Earned to Be Paid in Current Year" and "Payments Received in Current Year". Bold both entries.

2. In Row 3 add the column labels for each section. In Cells A3 through E3 those are "Month", "Income", "Source", "Currency", and "Paid". In Cells G3 through

K3 those are "Date Received", "Source", "Amount", "Tax Liab", and "For". Bold all entries.

3. In Rows 4 through 11 of Columns A through E add the text shown in the sample.

4. Use fill color to change Cell B9 to yellow fill. This is to indicate that that payment amount is an estimated amount and not yet finalized.

5. In Cell B14 type "Total Outstanding" and then Merge & Center Cells B14 through D14.

6. In Cells C15 through C20, list the currency abbreviations "USD", "CAD", "GBP", "EUR", "AUD", and "INR".

7. In Cell B21 add the text "USD Value" and then Merge & Center Cells B21 and C21.

8. In Cell B15 add a SUMIFS formula to sum all outstanding payments in Column B when the currency listed in Column D matches the currency in Cell C15 and Column E for that row is blank. Use dollar signs to fix the cell references so that you can copy the formula down for the other currencies.

   a. In our sample that is: =SUMIFS(B$4:B$13,D$4:D$13,C15,E$4:E$13,"")

   b. If you were willing to have the table be placed off to the side instead of directly below the entries, you could use column references instead of cell references. So you'd have =SUMIFS(B:B,D:D,O2,E:E,"") for a table located in Cells N1 through P8 where the USD in Cell C15 is now in Cell O2.

9. Copy the formula from Cell B15 to Cells B16 through B20.

   a. Because we used a cell reference for the currency value (C15 in the original formula) and dollar signs to fix our cell references the formula should auto-adjust for each currency but continue to reference the same range of cells.

10. Convert the values in Cells B15 through B20 to your currency. In this case that's USD, so the entries are:

    a. Cell D15: =B15

    b. Cell D16: =B16*0.799

    c. Cell D17: =B17*1.36

    d. Cell D18: =B18*1.205

    e. Cell D19: =B19*0.782

    f. Cell D20: =B20*0.016

11. Add a formula to Cell D21 to sum the values in Cells D15 to D20. In this case, =SUM(D15:D20)

12. Bold the cells in the top and bottom rows of the table as well as the currency abbreviations in the middle of the table.

13. Select the entire table and place All Borders on the cells and then place a Thick Box Border on the table. Select the top row and place a Thick Box Border on the top row. Select the bottom row and place a Thick Box Border on the bottom row.

14. In Cells G4 through K7 input information on payments received from the sample.

15. In Cell I10 add a sum formula to total the amount received to-date. In this case, =SUM(I4:I9)

16. In Cell J10 add a sum formula to total the amount of estimated taxes payable to date. In this case, =SUM(J4:J9)

That's it. As you add more entries, make sure that your formulas at the bottom update to include those new entries. As I mentioned above, you could move the summary table and the summation of amounts received off to the side and change the formulas to reference entire columns instead of cell ranges. But I usually just write my sum formulas so that they incorporate all of the rows up to the summary rows so that when I insert new rows, the formulas auto-adjust to include the newly inserted rows.

As mentioned above, if you're not dealing with multiple currencies, then you can just use a basic SUMIF formula to add all amounts earned that have not yet been paid. (Just keep in mind SUMIF and SUMIFS require you to enter your criteria in a different order.)

Okay. Now let's build a two-variable analysis grid.

TWO-VARIABLE ANALYSIS GRID
OVERVIEW

The two-variable analysis grid is an incredibly convenient tool for doing what-if analysis. What if you earn $15 per hour, how much more will you make in a month than if you earn $10 per hour? What if you can sell your house for $350,000 instead of $325,000? What if you can find a broker who will only charge you 4% for selling your house instead of 6%?

Basically, this grid takes any two variables, hours worked and pay per hour or home sale price and broker commission, and then calculates the possible outcomes. You can then take those outcomes and apply conditional formatting to them to see which combinations of the two variables result in outcomes that are "good" or "bad."

Let's walk through an example that looks at selling your home. Here it is:

	A	B	C	D	E
1					
2	Owe Now	$300,000.00			
3					
4	Sale Price	3%	4%	5%	6%
5	$325,000.00	$ 15,250.00	$ 12,000.00	$ 8,750.00	$ 5,500.00
6	$330,000.00	$ 20,100.00	$ 16,800.00	$ 13,500.00	$ 10,200.00
7	$335,000.00	$ 24,950.00	$ 21,600.00	$ 18,250.00	$ 14,900.00
8	$340,000.00	$ 29,800.00	$ 26,400.00	$ 23,000.00	$ 19,600.00
9	$345,000.00	$ 34,650.00	$ 31,200.00	$ 27,750.00	$ 24,300.00
10	$350,000.00	$ 39,500.00	$ 36,000.00	$ 32,500.00	$ 29,000.00
11					

First, in Cell B2 we list what you currently owe for the house. That's the mortgage you're going to have to pay off when you sell. (Which technically makes this a three-variable analysis, but the grid still only compares combinations of the two variables.)

Below the mortgage amount is a table that shows different potential house sales prices on the left-hand side and different broker commissions along the top. As discussed in *Budgeting for Beginners*, when you sell your house you won't get the list price. You'll get that list price minus what you have to pay the brokers on both sides of the deal to do the transaction. In my area that's a minimum of 3% and usually 6% so that's what I've used in the table.

What you then see in the table itself are the possible amounts you would take home after paying that broker commission and paying off the balance on the mortgage.

That formula for Cell B5 is =(A5*(1-B4))-B2

So, equals the sale price times 1 minus the commission rate and then that value minus your mortgage that you have to pay off.

I've also applied conditional formatting to the table to highlight when you will at least receive $15,000 from the sale (that's the green) and when you'll receive at least $30,000 from the sale (that's the blue).

So you could use this table to determine whether it was worth selling your house. If you need at least $15,000 to afford to move, then you can't sell the house for $325,000 if you're paying a 6% commission. You won't have enough. You could only sell for $325,000 if you're paying a 3% commission.

But at $350,000 you could pay any of the commission rates and still make enough on the sale for it to be worthwhile.

As I said above, these grids are great for any sort of two-variable analysis. I use them all the time when looking at number of units I need to sell at a given price to make a target income, potential consulting income at different hourly rates and hours worked per week, etc. Basically, as long as you're looking at only two variable inputs you can use a grid like this to see your potential outcomes.

So let's build this one.

TWO-VARIABLE ANALYSIS GRID
BUILD

As a reminder, this is what we're building:

	A	B	C	D	E
1					
2	Owe Now	$300,000.00			
3					
4	Sale Price	3%	4%	5%	6%
5	$325,000.00	$ 15,250.00	$ 12,000.00	$ 8,750.00	$ 5,500.00
6	$330,000.00	$ 20,100.00	$ 16,800.00	$ 13,500.00	$ 10,200.00
7	$335,000.00	$ 24,950.00	$ 21,600.00	$ 18,250.00	$ 14,900.00
8	$340,000.00	$ 29,800.00	$ 26,400.00	$ 23,000.00	$ 19,600.00
9	$345,000.00	$ 34,650.00	$ 31,200.00	$ 27,750.00	$ 24,300.00
10	$350,000.00	$ 39,500.00	$ 36,000.00	$ 32,500.00	$ 29,000.00
11					

To do so:

1. In Cells A2 and B2 add your current mortgage information. In the sample that's "Owe Now" and "$300,000".

2. Bold the values in those cells and then place All Borders and then a Thick Box Border around them.

3. In Cells A4 through E4 add the labels along the top of the table, "Sale Price", "3%", "4%", "5%", and "6%".

4. In Cells A5 through A10 add the labels along the side of the table, "$325,000", "$330,000", "$335,000", "$340,000", "$345,000", and "$350,000".

   a. In this case you could type $325,000 into Cell A5 and then use a formula in Cell A6 that adds $5,000 to that value and then copy the formula down the rest of the cells. (So Cell A10 would be =A9+5000)

5. In Cell B5 add the formula =($A5*(1-B$4))-B2

   a. By using the $ signs we ensure that the calculation continues to refer to Column A for the mortgage value and Row 4 for the broker commission as well as Cell B2 for the mortgage balance. That's what allows us to write the formula once only.

6. Copy the formula from Cell B5 to Cells B5 through E10.

7. Use the Conditional Formatting Highlight Cells Greater Than option on Cells B5 through E10 to apply a blue fill and font color to any cells with a value of $30,000 or more. (This will require custom formatting.)

8. Use the Conditional Formatting Highlight Cells Greater Than option on Cells B5 through E10 to apply a green fill and font color to any cells with a value of $15,000 or more. (This is an available formatting option from the dropdown menu.)

9. Bold the values in Column A and in Row 4 of the table.

10. Place an All Borders border around the entire table as well as a Thick Box Border.

11. Highlight just the cells in Row 4 of the table and place a Thick Box Border around them.

12. Highlight just the cells in Column A of the table and place a Thick Box Border around them.

That's it. You should now have a table that calculates potential payouts for a house sold at those prices and paying those commissions where the mortgage balance is $300,000. And that table should apply conditional formatting to the calculated values when they are either greater than $15,000 or greater than $30,000.

Hopefully you can see how easy it would be to change the inputs into the table to whatever you need. And how easy it is to expand the table to include more potential values. (If not, reach out. I'm happy to help. Speaking of, that's it so let's move on to the conclusion.)

CONCLUSION

So there you have it. How to create one single Excel workbook that summarizes all of the information you need to track your financial health. I hope it wasn't too overwhelming for you. It's a lot to take in. But once you get this up and running it's pretty straight-forward to use. Just update your numbers every couple of weeks and you'll be able to see where you are currently and what risks you might be facing in the future.

If you don't understand something or you get stuck putting any of this together, reach out to me. I'm always happy to answer questions. My email is mlhumphreywriter@gmail.com.

I don't check that email every single day but I do check it often and I will get back to you and am happy to answer any "how do I?" questions you might have.

And thanks for buying the book. You're on the right path to getting a handle on all of this, so don't give up now. You can do it. Just take it one step at a time. And don't hesitate to reach out if you get stuck.

APPENDIX A:

INPUTTING INFORMATION AND NAVIGATING EXCEL

Copying

To copy the contents of a cell(s), highlight what you want to copy, and use (1) Ctrl + C, (2) right-click and Copy, or (3) select Copy from the Clipboard section of the Home tab. Move to the new location and Paste.

Remember that when you copy a cell that contains a formula that the formula will adjust when moved and will no longer reference the same cells. If you need the cell references to remain the same, use a $ in front of the column and row references.

Delete Column or Row

To delete a row or column, highlight the entire row or column you want to delete by clicking on the row or column name, right-click, and select Delete.

Freeze Panes

If you want to be able to see the top row(s) of your worksheet or the left-most column(s) of your worksheet no matter where you are in the worksheet, then you want to use Freeze Panes. To freeze panes, click into the cell just below the rows you want to keep visible and just to the right of the columns you want to keep visible and then go to the View tab and choose Freeze Panes from the Freeze Panes dropdown menu.

Insert Cells

To insert a cell or cells into a worksheet, highlight the cell or cells where you want to insert, right-click, and select Insert. You can then choose to shift the existing contents of the worksheet down or to the right to accommodate the new cells.

Pasting

Once you have copied or cut an item, to paste it into a new location, use (1) Ctrl + V, (2) right-click and Paste, or (3) select Paste from the Clipboard section of the Home tab.

Use Paste Special to paste just values or to transpose the content.

APPENDIX B:

FORMATTING INFORMATION IN EXCEL

Bolding Text

To bold text, highlight the selected text or cell(s) and use (1) Ctrl + B, (2) click on the B in the Font section of the Home tab, or (3) right-click, choose Format Cells, go to the Font tab, and change the Font Style to Bold.

Borders

To place a border around a cell or cells, highlight the selected cells, and (1) click on the border dropdown in the Font section of the Home tab or (2) right-click, choose Format Cells, go to the Border tab, and choose the border you want to add.

Remember that if you want to change the color or the line type of the border from the default, do so before you choose your borders.

Cell Text Alignment

To change the alignment of the text within a cell or cells, highlight the cell(s), and then (1) in the Alignment section on the Home tab select the type of desired cell alignments (Top Align, Middle Align, Bottom Align and Align Left, Center, Align Right) or (2) right-click, choose Format Cells, go to the Alignment tab, and choose the desired Horizontal and Vertical alignment types from the dropdown menus.

Cell Text Orientation

To change the orientation of the text within a cell, highlight the cell(s), and then (1) in the Alignment section on the Home tab, choose your type of desired orientation from the orientation dropdown menu or (2) right-click, choose Format Cells, go to the Alignment Tab, and change the orientation from 0 degrees to the desired orientation by either clicking and dragging the orientation line or inputting your desired value in the Degrees field.

Currency Formatting

To format a cell as currency, select the cell(s) and (1) click on the $ sign in the Number section of the Home tab, (2) select Currency or Accounting from the dropdown menu in the Number section of the Home tab, or (3) right-click, choose Format Cells, go to the Number tab, and choose Currency or Accounting from the available list.

Date Formatting

To format a cell as a date, select the cell(s) and (1) select Short Date or Long Date from the dropdown menu in the Number section of the Home tab, or (2) right-click, choose Format Cells, go to the Number tab, and choose Date from the available list and then choose a date type from the box of examples.

Fill Color

To fill a cell with a specific color, select the cell(s) and (1) choose the color from the fill color dropdown menu in the Font section of the Home tab, or (2) right-click, choose Format Cells, go to the Fill tab, and choose a color.

Merge and Center

To merge a selection of cells and center your selected text across those cells, make sure the text you want to keep is in the top left-most cell of the selection, highlight the cells you want to merge, and click on Merge & Center in the Alignment section of the Home tab.

Number Formatting

To format a cell as a number, select the cell(s) and (1) click on the comma sign in the Number section of the Home tab, (2) select Number from the dropdown menu in the Number section of the Home tab, or (3) right-click, choose Format Cells, go to the Number tab, and choose Number from the available list. You can set the desired number of decimal places either in the Number section of the Home tab (using the 0.00 images with arrows next to them) or in the Format Cells dialogue box once you've chosen Number as your format type.

Percent Formatting

To format a cell as a percentage, select the cell(s) and (1) click on the % sign in the Number section of the Home tab, (2) select Percentage from the dropdown menu in the Number section of the Home tab, or (3) right-click, choose Format Cells, go to the Number tab, and choose Percentage from the available list.

Wrap Text

To wrap the text within a cell so that it flows onto multiple lines within the cell based upon the cell's width, highlight the cell(s) and (1) click on Wrap Text in the Alignment section of the Home tab, or (2) right-click, choose Format Cells, go to the Alignment tab, and check the Wrap text box.

APPENDIX C:

MATH, ANALYSIS, AND USING FORMULAS IN EXCEL

Addition

You can perform simple addition using the + sign or sum multiple values using the SUM ( ) function. For example =A1+B2 will add cells A1 and B2 together. Or =SUM(A1:A25) will sum cells A1 through A25.

Complex Formulas

Excel allows for complex formulas where more than one function is completed within a cell. When using complex formulas, be sure that you use parens properly because =A1+B2/C1 is different from =(A1+B2)/C1.

Conditional Formatting

Conditional formatting allows you to specify formatting for a cell or range of cells that will apply only when certain criteria are met. For example, you can have a cell turn red if the value falls below a certain threshold or green if it reaches a certain point. To apply conditional formatting, highlight the cell(s), go to the Styles section of the Home tab, and choose from the Conditional Formatting dropdown menu. In the example in this guide, the Highlight Cells Rules option was used.

Division

You can perform division using the / sign. For example, =A1/B2 will divide A1 by B2.

Filtering

If you have your data arranged with a header row and then the information listed in rows below that, you can filter your data to look at just those rows of data that meet certain criteria. To do so, click into the header row and choose Filter from the Sort & Filter dropdown in the Editing section of the Home tab. The filter will only work for contiguous columns. (So if you have a blank column in the middle of your header row, it will only allow filtering on columns to the left of the blank column or to the right of the blank column, but not on both at once.)

To choose your filter criteria, click on the arrow next to the column header. You can filter by using the checkboxes next to each listed value, by applying filtering criteria such as equals or contains, or by text or highlight color.

Holding a Cell Reference Constant When Copying a Formula

If you want to copy a formula but want to keep the reference to a cell constant, then you need to use the $ sign. For example, if you have a formula =(A3+B3)/C1 and you want to copy that formula so that the references to A3 and B3 change to reflect the row they're in, but keep the reference to Cell C1 constant, then you would write the formula as =(A3+B3)/C1. If you want to just keep the column reference constant, only put the $ sign in front of the letter portion of the cell reference ($C1). If you want to just keep the row reference constant, only put the $ sign in front of the number portion of the cell reference (C$1).

Multiplication

You can perform simple multiplication using the * sign or multiply many values using the PRODUCT( ) function. For example, =A1*B2 will multiply Cell A1 by Cell B2. Or =PRODUCT(A1:A25) will multiply Cell A1 by Cell A2 by Cell A3 through to Cell A25.

Sorting

Sorting allows you to display your information in a specific order. For example, by date, value, or alphabetically. You can also sort across multiple columns, so you can, for example, sort first by date, then by name, then by amount.

To sort your data, select all cells that contain your information, including your header row if there is one, and go to the Editing section of the Home tab. Click on the arrow next to Sort & Filter, and choose Custom Sort.

Your other option is to go to the Data tab and click on the Sort option there. Either path will bring you to the Sort dialogue box where you can set your sort options.

Subtraction

You can perform subtraction using the - sign. For example, =A1-B2 will subtract B2 from A1.

Appendix C

Using Quotation Marks In Formulas

Quotation marks are used in formulas to identify text. So in the following equation H2=”Full Price” is looking for a text match of Full Price within that cell.

=IF(OR(H2="Full Price", H2="Discounted",H2="Free"),
IF((M2+N2)>G2,"YES","NO"),"")

ABOUT THE AUTHOR

M.L. Humphrey is a former stockbroker with a degree in Economics from Stanford and an MBA from Wharton who has spent close to twenty years as a regulator and consultant in the financial services industry.

––––––––––––––––––––––––––

You can reach M.L. at mlhumphreywriter@gmail.com or at mlhumphrey.com.